Name: _____ Date: _____

School: _____

City/Location: _____

Dorm/Building Name: _____

Move in Date: _____ Graduation Year: _____

Classes Start Date: _____

Class Schedule:

_____

_____

_____

_____

Other Schools applied to:

_____

_____

What am I looking for in a college?

What do I think campus life will be like?

I'm setting three goals for this year, and they will be:

I am most nervous for:

I am most excited for:

I am making sure to pack:

Some items to bring that remind me of home are:

My packing list includes:

My packing list includes:

My packing list includes:

Some reasons I chose to study at my school are:

Moving in went like:

My first 24 hours after I arrived went like:

My first week went like:

My first impression of my new school is:

My living space can be described how:

What do I think about my dorm/building?

A funny encounter I have had so far is:

On a typical day, my dorm/building sounds like?

What I can see from my windows:

From my living space, I can hear:

Walking around campus I typically see/hear:

Having a roommate/neighbors is like?

I spent my first Friday night doing:

My first week went like:

My favorite class so far is:

Some people I have met so far are:

When I am having a moment or need time alone, I:

The best way I found to combat homesickness:

I kept in touch with my family by:

The biggest physical challenges I face:

The biggest emotional challenges I face:

A typical morning includes:

A typical evening includes:

My favorite place to eat on campus is:

My favorite food served on campus is:

My favorite snacks I keep in my room are:

My favorite and least favorite professors are:

My favorite and least favorite classes are:

What I enjoy doing most on the weekend is:

Have I been to any cool parties?:

Who are my favorite people I have met so far:

Have I picked up any new hobbies?

What does a typical homework assignment look like:

The latest I've stayed up working on a paper or homework was:

My visit home went like:

Holidays at school are like:

My second semester differs from my first semester because:

My friends and I like to hang out where on campus?

Our favorite off campus hang out is?

Some fun campus events I went to:

The best local stores are?

The best local restaurants are?

I do my best studying on campus at:

The typical weather at my school is:

Some clubs or activities I have joined are:

My grades are like:

I feel _____ about my major?

Have I gone on any dates?:

I hang out with _____ the most.

My favorite thing about my school is:

I probably need to vent about something, do it here.

Exams in college have me feeling like:

Finals studying involves:

The greatest friend I made helps me by:

End of the semester/Move out thoughts:

This year was _____?

Did my expectations become reality?:

If I could remember one memory forever in perfect detail from this year, what would it be?

What I loved about my Freshman year?

How I grew as a person:

Some things I did not love about my freshman year:

What lessons I have learned that I will take with me into Sophomore year:

Memory to Remember:

Memory to Remember:

Memory to Remember:

Memory to Remember:

Memory to Remember:

Memory to Remember:

Memory to Remember:

Memory to Remember:

Memory to Remember:

Memory to Remember:

Memory to Remember:

Memory to Remember:

Memory to Remember:

Memory to Remember:

Memory to Remember:

Memory to Remember:

Memory to Remember:

Memory to Remember:

Memory to Remember:

Memory to Remember:

Memory to Remember:

Memory to Remember:

Memory to Remember:

Memory to Remember:

Memory to Remember:

Notes:

Notes:

Notes:

Notes:

Notes:

Notes:

Notes:

Notes:

Notes:

Notes:

Tickets / Memorabilia:

Tickets / Memorabilia:

Tickets / Memorabilia:

Tickets / Memorabilia:

Tickets / Memorabilia:

Tickets / Memorabilia:

Photos:

Photos:

Photos:

Photos:

Photos:

Photos:

Photos:

Manufactured by Amazon.ca
Acheson, AB